HAUNT

(NO-BOUNDARY PROPOSALS)

HAUNT

(NO-BOUNDARY PROPOSALS)

Keith Waldrop

"...though I give my body..."

Instance Press

Some of these poems first appeared in *Avec, Blue Mesa, Brøndums Encyklopaedi, Epoch, Hodos, Inscape,* and *Lingo.*

Potential Random was published as a chapbook by Gale Nelson at Paradigm Press.

Cover art by Keith Waldrop
Cover design by Leonard Brink

ISBN 0-9679854-0-4
LCCN 00 132506

Instance Press
P.O. Box 3124
Saratoga, CA 95070
www.poetrypress.com/instance

Instance Press books are available from Small Press Distribution.

CONTENTS

for Paol Keineg

INDICATION

"The sole true Something — This!"

I

> I look for the
> word worth a thousand
> pictures, perhaps akin
> to OHG *botahha*
> tub, vat, cask

> the form of the root
> unknown, origin
> human or divine

∎

Is there anything but this?

∎

From somewhere, I have copied down:

> "the sleeper constructs this whole wide world, and himself
> becomes its doomsday"

From somewhere, the impulse to construct a monument. A tomb. Or, rather,
to redesignate the world – mark it as a gravestone.

From somewhere, a generation of erasures.

∎

(There is no universe.)

∎

> and Aquinas: body the
> product of soul

the parts of the
body contained
in the soul

imperfect unless
what is enfolded in the
soul be

unfolded in the body

■

lost information

■

limited by
clocks on earth, but a
wealth of words
for darkness

■

collapsed body

■

sword
dogs
fowl
and *what* beasts of the earth?

■

A word will not come to mind.

Maybe not *yet* a word.

■

From the corner, I arrive at the far corner, go back along the walk to where my
walk began. Is the house still there?

(From here.)

I ponder this.

                              ■

                    (no *early*
                    universe) dancer
                    wearing too many
                    clothes

                    (*or* late)

                    earth its diseases, in a small
                    voice, like a child's — how
                    dreaming is related to
                    the *depth* of sleep

                        ■

                        enfolded, death
                        at the window, un-

                        folded, blue
                        starlight, with traces
                        of metal

                        ■

                    first *love,* says
                    Montherlant, then
                    work, then *nothing*

no doubt he meant life
in three stages, I think
we suffer them
all at once

together
like

this

■

beware (I
say –
and here, with all these
words, I
make no sound) – be-

ware spring breezes

II

simple connections involving
a physical law

nameless
objects seen
imperfectly

tiddlywinks or
the catapult

inadequacy of pictures

he believed the
music but mis-
heard the message

simple connections involving a
ping-pong ball

■

noisy poem of
earth and its diseases

violet, cannonading
into blue

■

failure of
memory, a nothing
thing

path of an object launched
by a sling

contrary
to predictions, will

not participate in the
soul's

this

four oblique
paths, involving
three different directions

why from
six
to twelve?

what happens
to the ball?

why travel
across circles?

why
sing of the soul?

the concept of reversibility

■

to consecrate (to
prepare for battle)

a fixed floor
required

consciousness in
slippage

to lower
the dead

from a pointlike source
all monsters, all
humanity

∎

To hear "Why I left the Communist Party," an admission charge of twenty-five cents.

∎

why do we
understand so late what
happens

does not happen

∎

to make the bear move

moving my hands
moving my arms, feet, legs

my head

III

[INCIDENTAL MUSIC]

> according to the records I was
> born in December (I know
> lots of other things I don't
> remember)

∎

> walking from
> heaven saw her
> riding, water in

> her hand, upon a milk-white
> steed various
> shapes

> asp adder and a
> bolt of red-hot iron

∎

The road we imagine spectres to walk, concealed in illegible documents or the roar of post office trucks—when they fail to appear, the spectres, we ourselves go out along that road, unmoored and angry.

We think we travel west—due west—but straight ahead of us, in time, the sun starts up.

∎

In time.

∎

Ah, said a king named Wise, had *I* but been there to advise, the Creation would have fewer mistakes.

■

the step to *three*

■

what kind of story can *I*
tell — the light
falls as it always fell

■

localized rescue

ocean at outer
rim her-

maphroditic
ocean lost

■

He lifts his eyes — I watch him — to be burnt out by the sun.

■

... to work towards restoration of the original horror — as if a nurse should mourn for
every patient

■

just when I think I know
this from that, old
bottles turn into
Buddhas — just when I

think I've got things
down pat
a cat
jumps through the judas

■

Private money, a contradiction in terms. But all *my* payment.

■

Forlorn (and my only) hope, shifty maneuver, somehow *to outwit the historical dynamic.*

■

the moon is dry, the moon is
stark—half of it lit up the
other half dark

one side on display, the
other doesn't show—nobody
lives there, nothing
seems to grow

■

a weird light to
wake in, brightness like a
ladder up and

on and I
wanted to jot down here
how the shadows were gone

so many verbs

irregular

the point, my pencil, broken

■

in the blazing
sun, it was all like
grace

(*until the red sea parts again*)

amazing

■

my prison empty, my
prisoners

gone free — now that no one's under
lock and key

who will remember me?

■

I will need to go out
soon and build
a ballad to the moon

■

Setting out... an extended journey...

Hardly around the corner, I encounter this.

IV

While you were listening to "With the Face Uncovered," I was hearing "Cortical Gray."

While I visualized, you were making yourself at home.

While you believed, I trembled.

While we were unavailable, I was without.

V

[ONE BREATH]

CANTATA
CONTAINING A LINE BY MAYAKOVSKY

1

how recently the world
was ice

ach says
he the physical
world nature's

dead
soul

terrible pre-
occupation chasing
the east

wind struggle of
sun to cross the sky

to make a garden and
pools of water
should I with

a word (any
word says

Socrates) bring to a
halt
becoming

what has been
done under the

sun is terrible what
is wanting un-
accountable

we sleep says
somebody in order to

forget *I*
remember
sleep

idea by idea my
body regains its

argument singers
of both
sexes instruments

of many sorts
music for the

deaf ear pictures
for the blind
roll call in the Trojan horse

to sit is to possess to
sit again is to reside

2

nymphs
lovers
invisible singers
angels (believing)
despairing lovers
the self unhoused, positionless

if the telephone
rings
in a room where
no one is, is there

a sound

is there a ring, a
caller, is
there a telephone

■

Eleanor cries out

■

groove into neural groove
evidence
of hemispheres

pure tone con-
firmed pure
tone

(my beautiful

exhausted

army)

■

*Eleanor gives out a soft
cry*

■

the strongest beat re-

quires

interval — I cannot
lift the piano

a stone falls near me, a stone
common to this

area

over the extension
of things, a
camouflage of color

■

*Eleanor just raising a
cup of tea to her
lips suddenly*

cries out

3

vertical the rain
sleeps rivers run
dry a sound

too fine to be
heard

after-
thought re-
tracing small

volumes but when un-
folded

after dread come
sorrows
soon

the thumb the big
toe and the left

ear a sympathetic
tree among
the weeds

walking from
heaven saw her

her hand various
local
shapes bagatelles

of the higher life correct
mourning in-

habited arabesques
narrative of
my mishaps

knowledge which
remains un-

thought sun getting
brighter certain stars
older

than the universe
between

slag and
bloom go and *see* or
wait and see

notions simple and
surrounded

4

Chorale:

I lift my eyes
I fix my gaze
on paradise

I paraphrase

VI

"And I remember myself to have remembered..."
        —Saint Augustine

He assumes that what once was, no longer exists, certain that what is to come, has yet to exist. And, true enough, he lives, as one must, in his now.

But he fudges.

Time: he turns it. He twists it this way and that. He would, if he knew how, stop time, reverse time, turn time inside out.

Since he and the world cannot exist together,

the world retreats.

       ■

    I would not haul you
    here, out of the past, you my

    disturbing news

    the dead each
    age buried
    deeper and deeper

    dreams from after-
    images, failed
    after-dreams

    gregarious galaxies

involved, intellectual, in-
constant

■

after the fall of the
city—bull-fights, hawking
parties, games of tennis

love, comforted with
curious gifts, denied
pepper

(the eggs are counted)

feather-headed as we
are—frenzy
of hate

to empty the coffers *in
time,* a
hoop of gold
to assist

pathetic letter, many
diverting reflections wishing
all happiness to love, great

distress her
white breast powdered
with jewels—the little
drama

opens

■

hitherto, quiet
river, now winding

channel, dangerous
straits, rushing current

eddy

rapids

whirlpool

lotus

(thorny shrub which grows in abundance along the shores of the Sea of Galilee)

■

To go *straight to her,* with a present.

But he cannot think how to do it.

Not that she "has everything." Merely that his fist is clenched.

And the local, with her, seems of no influence. He has, in short, nothing to give her.

And, besides, there are *no straight lines.*

■

CHAOS = complete disorder. Which is to say, a fantasm of the disciplined mind, a contrary image created for purposes of orientation, something to justify excessive demand for clarity.

There is no chaos.

■

here is the city — lie
down

large chart, to the
horizon damaged difficult
characters

map
larger than the territory

curvature to
distinguish the end
from the beginning

perhaps not
meant for me
this

■

not a blossom on the earth, no
shadow come to maturity

east and west, sunrise
and seashore

altars, ovens
ruined city, the ruins

of cities, wealth
parallel to darkness

■

Remember:

1. cool garden

2. funereal rest

3. ripe years

4. the princely mule

5. eschatological feast

6. some cheap and hasty chance

7. suitable dignity

8. the wind blowing stark

9. women with shaven heads

10. aurora

11. a dada dado

12. generous extravagance, later, at the bombardment

13.   Adam's housecat

14.   snore and rumors of snore

15.   dangerous path, dangerous

■

I used to think there were two kinds of ghost: the haunter who seeks us out, possesses, infests — and the ghost who comes when bidden, our invited guest.

Invalid distinction. All ghosts are terrible.

All are called.

■

EVERYTHING = not simply whatever is, but a *total* of what is. The notion of a *uni*verse, the notion that there is one actual and one only.

This silly notion is bolstered by a sillier yet, to wit, that whatever we do not know, "therefore" does not exist.

There is no universe.

There is no everything.

■

in my search for the
insoluble, noisy
soul ın a
quiet church

the same, the
other, and something
in between, divisions

upon a ground, the
beauty of reminders

garment of soul or
mind as vessel

unity of
a broken consort

■

Horror does not necessarily result from a major transgression, some tremendous fault on the part of the horrified. It may arise from a trivial — an unconscious — failing, a lapse of etiquette at a moment when nothing seemed at stake.

Yes, seem*ed*: Horror is always already the past, irrevocable. Horror is a past overtaking, threatening to engulf the never completed present, canceling the future, becoming the future.

Lifeline on a severed hand.

■

again, with "no idea of
repetition implied"

■

This, lying now across my living lifeline, is the skull of a jay. Plumage gone — the brilliant blue, the crest — along with wings, beak, fierce stance, shrill scold (and also that uncanny call, as if electronic, the same bird makes in earliest morning).

The bone, like that of any bird, next to weightless, thin to translucence.

Smaller than one might expect from the living creature. In my palm, as nothing.

But this.

■

blue geranium golden
globe-flower wild
raspberry bird-
cherry with its tassels

how many chimneys

in a dying world
'difficult' for many
reasons, such factors as

physical danger,
economy, topography, climate,
availability and status of
personnel *and*
the political situation

disaster or battle conditions, planned but
isolated environments, sophisticated
hospitals, extreme
urgency

in un
certain
locations

■

Brought up along the clickety-clack of rails, we lack a sense of death, supposing it regularly rescheduled, rerouted, on some other line, another — later — track.

■

Sentimental stories, as of saints dying in rapture.

■

NOTHING = utter absence. Definable only by a complete catalog of what was or is or might be — the most tempting of all concepts.

There is no nothing.

■

average breath about a
pint of air, fifteen to twenty
times per minute, on

beyond dead
space, into the lungs

dying

■

The term 'irreversible.'

Useful.

■

Of substances required for life, oxygen — the most vital — least possible to store in the body.

■

December
notions

Between the Straits

"mine eye, mine eye..."
—Jeremiah

1

still seeking
delay

out of
harbor, indis-
tinguishable from
distance

ocean our
world, we
live on its terraces

fire as a
river, mud
flowing as fire

bad
dream and the
room in shadow

2

tried I might
remember that or
this — well,

things "of
moment" soul
in the form of a
flame, sorry
history of

faint blue galaxies

3

Jacob for his ravished
daughter Jacob
for his
son Benjamin

the virgins for
Jephthah's daughter

Israel for the death
of Samson David for Saul and
Jonathan

David for Abner

4

dark sky day
dark

5

upturned soil under lowering
sky hand-
fuls of seed — well,

clouds
bristle with
storm, meaning

spills across
mind, dark over
all the earth

6

last body the
body at last
a clod a

stench the flight of
self to

more important signs

artificial grace, almost
a stranger less
innocent more discerning

dainty shoes, glad
he had not sat down

8

men who have not
valued their lives an in-
delible
mark

huddled, a suggestion
of weight

gathered in her
left hand, begins
to act

conditioned by
lapse of time and
all I have — well,

liable to
trouble, shameful

that habit of laughter to
kill

distant remote telescopic far off faraway wide of stretching to yon yonder

10

in gorges space en-
throned, angels and
crocodiles

by-products of
the fire

pitch for the ark

11

and here they lie

bodies

sleeping

12

at the true
point where what
"is"
is what "seems"

13

all details, individual
elements

complex picture un-
seen, shadows

detaching, death
in districts

death at large

14

but hold your eye for
darkness, rivers
do not flow forever

space itself
fiery

15

contingency, deep
trench
blind

across palisades

if therefore some-
one should say

17

sore in the
night, tears on her
cheek

none to comfort her — well,

treacherous
friends, enemies, no
rest

18

stones, bones, the
shaft of an arrow

sticks, cube-shaped
chunks of clay, probably

small stone or
pebble

19

large letters for an empty name

20

fire in my
bones, a
net for my feet

desolate, faint
and — well,

new every morning

21

I am not
known in the
street, perhaps

once
there and I
inhabit that past

is it
nothing to you

22

in reference to
land never
sighted

gate, paving
stones

signal

movement of imaginary
islands

chartless

water

flowers

water

if in a
dream the so-called
conscious

organism if in
dreams
the shadow of a

body if

sense selects as
of a galaxy of
galaxies no
interest in the
past behind us, if there is

another way of saying this

24

for good, for
ever so long

25

then there are currents

POTENTIAL RANDOM

"...in deep sleep, the mind may come closest to perfecting rational thought. We have no reason for asserting the opposite, except that when we wake we do not remember our idea."

—Immanuel Kant

for Barbara Guest

I

alight
settle down
make a stop
linger

the alighting of birds

through a place
pass
dance wandering women
rebel
(unstable)

pinched off from a piece of clay

a kind of earth or soil
weakness
rejection

asphalt in the third millenium

unconscious recipient of mercy

caulking for Noah's ark
the basket in which Moses was placed

and the Nile

dependent on water
solemn
set up camp

(watch me disappear)
unafraid

filled with terror

fat
shelter
rest
be quiet

II

Many books have been destroyed, carelessly or by design. Lost, burnt, forgotten, volumes drop out of existence, along with—more easily disposed of—proofs never pulled, unpublished manuscripts, notes for books, plans and proposals for things to be written, collected, put into books. The number of projects unaccomplished in history must be enormous.

And much larger, almost infinite, the realm of projects unattempted, never started, what no one ever thought to try.

My doctrine would derive, not from wisdom concealed by anxious arhats in caves beneath impassable Himalayas, nor from a chain of unwritten instruction passed guru-wise down centuries. It would remain in a world beneath notice, too obvious to be considered. Thus, secret.

The world as it lies open here, waiting for me to fail.

I do not need to know your real name.

This much seems obvious, that as we move along the path, slowly but certainly the path replaces us. And also, just as strands in the vitreous humour cloud the visual field, words stray, making our thought opaque.

III

Ship is in danger, ship
must be repaired, but ship must
continue afloat as long as we continue
crossing the dangerous waters.

  ■

These events take place in order that they may be represented.

  ■

Egypt is memory, captivity in Egypt
is memory. Ship of the
North with its
anchor from the South, it rides above the Ur-Fish.

  ■

From many names for God come
many gods. If you believe in any,
you may know how the body could be glorified.

  ■

And if you will rise with that
withered arm...

  ■

Names of things
can never enter Heaven.

  ■

Turn now, together with your body — turn
past the five windows, past
your pride in the dark image and your
body turning.

  ■

Waking, doomsday for some dream.

■

Words perish, like the word for oyster. Words
are a great retreat — they are
like strips of existing or like
sea-shells echoing words.

IV

A view of the landscape.

up

A view of the river, of
bathers along the bank.

down

Now a view of the view, a
sheer perspective.

charmed

He is sent away, so
begins to exist.

strange

Homeward bound taxi: rather hazy idea.

top (or truth)

Surely he'll find something to
say on the silliness of opera.

bottom (or beauty)

V

Stand here, where without too great a turn, my eyes meet your eyes mirrored. And my eyes in the mirror, your eyes.

Whatever's to either side of us runs out of the frame and is lost. What's behind us is lost behind us.

Reduced to picture, we can appreciate our picture, reversed but right side up. Our lines of sight are straightforward — the surface glassy, clear.

Simple and astonishing, the location of bodies, grandly irregular in the smooth surrounding echo.

VI

wicked at first
tore their clothes
refusing to speak
took off their sandals

■

I know not what

■

fasted
ready by tomorrow
gashed themselves
exactly at midnight
freely lamented

■

I know not whither

■

wept

VII

What is seen then, as the center, is not the center, but only light feeding into the center.

Devastation, ritual of covenant accompanied by darkness.

Wash your clothes.

Shave off your hair.

Bathe yourself in water.

All space becomes neutral.

Uncaulked and unprovisioned, we reach shore.

Something must be done about darkness before we can live in this light.

Cold air and warm air twinkle the starlight, Nobody's mother tongue.

VIII

At the mouth of the stream, there is a mysterious island.
A mountain on the island.
The trees there bear (no Tree-of-Life) precious stones.
A place of desires.

I crouch down in my torn clothes.
Bloodstained cloak.
I cut off my hair and howl.
Slain man wallowing in his blood.

They are so terrified they forget to call for mourners.
The other side of death.
They mourn with astonishing frequency.
A razor from beyond the Euphrates.

She saunters under quick green trees, angels falling around her.
Chinks in the rational.
Song turns into lamentation.
Canopy of darkness.

Soldiers offer strawberry coral.
Eidola.
The dark is slippery.
Shapeless logs, sacred stones, then images.

IX

The shapes of things rise up against me—cube, pyramid, cone—actual, ideal—
and threaten to trip me up, obstruct me, box me in.

■

They lie in wait. They spring from my own eyes.

■

I take them all, straight-lined or curved, reducing each to a circle—closed, each
circle, by a movement of my hand.

X

No counting the
number of the dead, the number
of those who will die.

Kant thought Earth had at one time, like Saturn, a ring. Composed of watery vapors, it encircled the world in beauty, to be regarded and appreciated by Earth's inhabitants.

In the course of time, from the action of a comet or other cause, the waters composing that ring were loosed and fell upon Earth and in that deluge the greater part of a sinful mankind perished.

Lost thereby, for the survivors, which is to say, for us: the sight of that ring in the upper air, the most exquisite view from the surface of Paradise or a young planet—our rainbow a faint reminder of the glory lost.

At the center of every
system is a flaming
body.

Bright sun between
grapevine and fig tree.

By coincidence,
sun and moon
are exactly the same size.

Celestial phenomena—there are
so many stars—merge along
my line of sight.

Directly before my eye descends
a spider—slowly, a ways
away, just down to eye-level.

Earth spins in the
sun's corona.

High countries in the
dust, and also
elephants, alas.

A hundred miles of
umbra over un-
counted acres of tundra.

I try to find some
sense in which behind is
not in back of.

It suggests the
idea of a bird.

Monstrous colors on
certain things.

Monstrous things in
uncertain colors.

One has to choose between
life
and what life contains.

Sunspots freeze in place.

Traveling some current, the
road imponderable.

Wastrel and hangman
thrive in the conquered
city.

What have I ever wanted to
say, but
how at this moment

XI

He walks in darkness, sits in darkness, dwells. Darkness falls, clouds, covers.

Or clouds of insects.

Or extinguishing a lamp.

After so many years, it ought to be infinite, but it never is and car lights glide so easily across his ceiling.

Neither cornlands, nor well-kept vineyards, only...

He cannot decide whether it's better to regard the soul as asleep or to take what seems like dream to be the waking world.

Scattered objects must have something to tell. Between the stars, between the positive particles, there is said to be "nothing" — can he hold this?

Delicate arms, bare, a hopeless gesture.

He cannot decide if cosmic fire creates the universe or ignites as executioner. The bitten line is broken, resembling lightning in a mediocre sky.

He cannot decide whether it is a friend in a dream speaking to him of danger, or a dangerous dream instructing him to act for the sake of the hypnotist.

His face darkens, with the darkness of delight.

He dreams a costume dream. What colors are latent in his darkness?

He does know that there are other shadows — uncertainties, headlights, fires on the beach at Nice, the horror of being chosen.

At moments life is so transparent that everything seems real, seems anyway familiar, distantly, like the aging face of someone he last saw young.

He cannot tell if his dream — so quickly forgotten — roused this storm in his soul, or if anxiety springs from his being awake, alert, dreamless.

...sallow throng beside dismal pool...

A very high and concave roof. He cannot decide where reason ends, associating as he does darkness with creation.

Between now and now, was time — will time be — empty?

What runs in the dark, or in daylight from stone to stone, sudden as spasm, a streak of blood?

Sheer throb relaxes into the mirror opposite, hard to follow, complex but quite complete. Losing certain colors might impoverish his visual life, but he realizes that a flaw in the numerical system would weaken the structure of the world.

With sunrise comes battle.

How is it, sensitive to signs of the times, he finds it so hard to decipher headlines?

And in what body would he like to be raised?

He is no more present to himself than objects in his view — the journey, long for so short a life, promising agate, chalcedony. He attends to changing expression, flickers of shadow, to keep his thought from running inward to inward light.

He cannot decide whether to change the subject.

He sings English and understands it is not always possible to make clear distinctions.

Sees no cause, he, to do no otherwise.

He considers movement, perhaps in the sense of change, honing the sword.

He cannot decide whether to describe his death in terms of hunger and sundown — or like a new-born babe, in the course of its disaster.

There have been some more overwhelmed than he with shame, with pity and terror — the east ablaze, the city's spires afire.

He cannot decide if the experiment is local, all life composed on this periphery, or if along the wall of stars there's by chance another creature — farther than faintest signals — signifying.

XII

Now a warm wind riffles
the leaves, ransacks the neighborhood.

∎

You will not wake up for me.

∎

In a certain chord, by the western loop of
Ermine Street, tomorrow
is well known, speckling as it does
flagstone and flag, slim white hands.

∎

The street ripples, roars. Take
it all away, lay it among
the scarcely remembered.

∎

As we stroll, a thick crust
underfoot and perfectly firm, beautiful
eyes and
teeth flashing.

∎

Moss may
edge the brook, tree-shaded
streets sleep, shadow-damaged, under
a late sun.

∎

Snakes hate summer and are
revived by rain.

∎

Housetops glitter a long-forgotten
flame, a frightful dream. But do not
ever dream of ghosts: they will undo
your remembering.

■

Lateen shades, lace curtains, rich
tumuli, the stillest city
swarms with hurry.

■

Our restless fingers, so they
stand. Throbbing
silence, darkening room.

■

Irrelevant, my own attire blood-
stained and ragged, what
nightmare sleeping or
awake, prying the bolted scuttle.

■

Otherwise, no signal for fear.

■

No sea-sickness in heaven.

■

Reality, Aristotle says, is not
a daytime serial.

■

Then comes Love's
army, disemboweled, Love's own
cavalry, guts
hanging from the saddle.

■

Adventures on my pillow and
below the snow-line.

■

A fierce pride
blazes at any
hint of earthly pleasure.

XIII

tall grain
food for the dead

a contest with uncleanness
detestable things

desire

thought

wallow in ashes
wail aloud
howl
scream

covering cherub

ideas of death

XIV

An aging house, well yes he
understands that — but suddenly
down it falls.

   ■

And he is in a garden.

   ■

And there are animals.

   ■

And he is in a garden and
there are trees.

   ■

And there are stones on
fire.

   ■

And, well, he walks
up and down on them.

   ■

But this is
the Hebrew *and,* not
a conjunction, merely some un-
translatable particle.

   ■

Cenotaph (there is no
body here).

   ■

(Somehow can't imagine
digging a separate grave for the heart.)

   ■

And everything is cast
down—plants, animals,
garden, stones, fire, Tyre
with its river called
Litany—along with himself.

   ■

The living organism, he
hears, is a
symbol of the psyche.

   ■

Thinking is inward seeing.
So Wittgenstein thought, and also
Swedenborg.

   ■

Die, well yes he knows he
has to, but thinks of it as being
killed—or killing.

   ■

As if at a distance—he
lives, not in
life, but across from it.

   ■

And it comes to pass.

   ■

And he tries to distinguish
life and its contents.

And they wheel around him, the cars, as
if he were standing still.

XV

Three lists remain: The first
is a list of the living,

who are now dead. The second records
the saints and martyrs, those

who laid down their lives to
be with Jesus. They fly to Him,

to miss the long repose.
The third list

is a list of the dead.

XVI

The days fan out, free and fragmentary, leaving him night — night folded around him and also inevitable unfolding night.

He is not absolutely sure the heavenly bodies are capable of desire.

Low decorative screens that he adores for their design conceal household gods and other holy objects.

He thinks of Moses, prepared to slay the death-angel.

Or Pisgah.

Love, in its mountain ranges.

Transhuman.

In earlier travels, he saw red windblown sand.

He has been told that the number of stars in the sky, whatever it is, is just the right number.

Also, that before he goes away again, he should file a change of address. There is no bravery more stubborn than this: the dead lie where they fall.

But note, he does not tell us, or even himself, everything. And, besides, this world lasts only so long as it lacks balance — the veer preserves us.

Passing regiments, glittering steel, outcurving flame, incoherent pollen. Note also, this poem is quite impersonal.

Hints reach him that stars of an earlier generation, crumbled to dust, haunt all the corridors.

Loath to part from his early life — or its aftertaste — trailing thus through nothing to nothing.

Cascades of unbound hair.

Ineffable cushions.

He can never manage to distinguish death's three weapons: a song, a dance, and whatever is absolutely pointless.

Hills surround abscissa, ordinate, simplest functions, the light too strong for more intricate patterns.

And among these secular representations, uncomfortable laughter.

In the shadow of the house, the tree. Then distant shots, a hollow roar. Traditional bonfires blaze on hilltops. Wrecked cafés across rainfilled streets. Glass-littered sidewalks.

This room, this door, this valley open on all sides, quick with the terror of choosing.

...eyeless sockets...

...fire-ravaged hair...

He cannot keep in mind how any thought left to itself, any autonomous act of the brain, is terrible — destruction if awake — asleep, a revelation — or even how the ligature of bones runs fast as lightning in the night.

His dream no longer upsets him — outlying barrows, cold, clustered, as if there really were a god of the cold — until he notices it is in color.

He cannot decide whether to wish for day or to wish for a day's return or to wish for a decision.

The last moment, here, now, reflected, sliding to its fade — he looks forward to it, such as it was.

He has been spared, on more than one occasion, unreasonable happiness.

XVII

augury
witchcraft
blob-like clouds
a pagan or a foreign hairstyle

∎

I adapt this to the apprehension of humankind.

∎

a circle or something that can be rolled
light-years from the center
round
inner rim of the disc of clouds
wheel
heavily processed inside stars
the wheel of a chariot
the central cluster
a round thistle
five billion years
wheel at the cistern

∎

And also to the understanding of angels.

∎

tightly packed stars
dwelling place of demons
dust warmed by the stars
haunt of jackals
the surrounding gas
without inhabitant

Keith Waldrop lives in Providence, Rhode Island, where he teaches at
Brown University and, with Rosmarie Waldrop, edits Burning Deck Press. He is
the translator of *The Selected Poems of Edmond Jabes*, as well as works by
Claude Royet-Journoud, Anne-Marie Albiach, Pascal Quignard and Dominique
Fourcade, among others. He is the author of numerous collections of poetry
and has received fellowships from the National Endowment for the Arts and
DAAD (Berlin). A selection of prose, *Hegel's Family*, was published in 1989 by
Station Hill Press. Recent books include *Light While There is Light* (Sun and
Moon), *The Opposite of Letting the Mind Wander* (Lost Roads), *The Locality
Principle*, and *The Silhouette of the Bridge* (both from Avec Books).